GET A JOB

AT THE
HOSPITAL

JOE RHATIGAN

Created and produced by
Bright Futures Press, Cary, North Carolina
www.brightfuturespress.com

Published by
Cherry Lake Publishing, Ann Arbor, Michigan
www.cherrylakepublishing.com

Photo Credits: Cover (left), megaflopp/Shutterstock; cover (middle), Suzanne Tucker/Shutterstock; cover (right), Ake Sak/Shutterstock; page 4, Rob Hainer/Shutterstock; page 5, Robert Przbysz/Shutterstock; page 7 (top), Sean Locke Photography/Shutterstock; page 7 (bottom), Poprotskiy Alexey/Shutterstock; page 9, Kameel4u/Shutterstock; page 11 (top), Zimmytws/Shutterstock; page 11 (bottom), thailoei92/Shutterstock; page 13, Richard Semik/Shutterstock; page 15 (top), Monkey Business Images/Shutterstock; page 15 (bottom), Zurijeta/Shutterstock; page 17, Brian A Jackson/Shutterstock; page 19 (top), Ryan Fletcher/Shutterstock; page 19 (bottom), Syda Productions/Shutterstock; page 21, Vadim Kozlovsky/Shutterstock; page 23 (top) sciencephoto/Shutterstock; page 23 (bottom), Fer Gregory/Shutterstock; page 25, Maksym Dykha/Shutterstock; page 27, wavebreakmedia/Shutterstock.

Illustrated by Chris Griffin

Library of Congress Cataloging-in-Publication Data

Names: Rhatigan, Joe, author.
Title: Get a Job at the hospital / by Joe Rhatigan.
Description: Ann Arbor, Michigan : Cherry Lake Publishing, [2016] | Series:
    Get a Job | Audience: Grade 4 to 6. | Includes index.
Identifiers: LCCN 2016006911| ISBN 9781634719070 (hardcover) | ISBN
    9781634719537 (pbk.) | ISBN 9781634719308 (pdf) | ISBN 9781634719766
    (ebook)
Subjects: LCSH: Hospitals--Juvenile literature. |
    Hospitals--Employees--Juvenile literature. | Hospital care--Juvenile
    literature. | Medical care--Juvenile literature.
Classification: LCC RA972.5 .R43 2016 | DDC 362.11--dc23
LC record available at http://lccn.loc.gov/2016006911

Printed in the United States of America

TABLE OF CONTENTS

Nobody wants to go to a hospital.

Going to the hospital usually means you're really sick. Or injured. Or in need of **surgery**. Or tests. Or treatments. And none of those things are much fun.

Fortunately, there are lots of people who want to work at hospitals. It's where they find opportunities to help and heal others. It's also a place where many people find rewarding careers.

This is very good news. When you do go to the hospital as a patient, it's nice to have trained professionals waiting to take care of you.

This is especially good news for people like **J**eremiah **O**liver **B**aumgartner. His initials are J.O.B., so his friends call him Job for short. Job's parents think it's the perfect nickname because, um, the kid can be a lot of work. It's not that Job tries to cause trouble. Disaster just seems to follow him around. He is accident prone and, as a result, makes frequent hospital visits.

Even though Job is not real, he's here to help you explore the real world of work. Tough luck for him, but good luck for us.

Let's follow Job around the hospital and meet the people who help him—and his family—out.

HEALTH BIT
Nearly 6 million people work in U.S. hospitals.

Whoa! Hope he got to eat the popsicle first!

I need to go to the *hospital* for a **SORE THROAT?!**

Most kids get sore throats at one point or another.

After a few days of rest, their throats get better. Not Job. He would get over one sore throat, only to wake up the next day with a new sore throat.

Not only was he having trouble eating and sleeping, but worst of all, he sounded like a frog. A sick frog. His family doctor told him he had **tonsillitis** and he would need to go to the hospital for an operation.

"I won't sound like a frog anymore, will I?" Job asked.

"Of course not," the doctor answered. "I know you're a little scared, but don't worry, you toadily won't croak."

"Ha-ha, very punny," Job said.

Before any test, treatment, or operation, a patient has to meet with an **admissions representative**. This person's job is to gather information from patients and tell them what to expect from their stay at the hospital. The representative makes sure patients are who they say they are, collects their insurance information for payment, and helps fill out lots of paperwork (there is always lots of paperwork!) Then the patient is given an identification bracelet with the patient's name and information on it.

The **pre-operative (Pre-op) nurse** gets the patient ready for surgery. This nurse checks the patient's vital signs (blood pressure and heartbeat) and makes that person comfortable. The pre-op nurse provides a dressing gown for the patient to wear. Then it's time to start an intravenous line (IV), which is a needle leading to a tiny tube inserted in the patient's vein. This sends medicine needed for the operation right into the patient's blood! Once everything is ready, the pre-op nurse moves the patient to the operating room.

Getting an IV isn't as scary as it looks.

During an operation, an **anesthesiologist** keeps patients comfy during their **surgery**. Depending on the surgery, the patients might stay awake and receive numbing medication so they can't feel anything. Or the patient is put to sleep. Either way, the patient feels no pain during the operation. The anesthesiologist stays with the patient during the entire operation to monitor their care.

The person with the scalpel is the **surgeon**. This doctor performs operations in order to treat diseases and injuries. Surgeons often specialize in certain parts of the body, such as the heart, the brain, the skin, or the throat.

"Scalpel, please!" Specially trained nurses assist surgeons during surgery.

The **recovery nurse** may be the same pre-op nurse who helped the patient get ready for the operation. The recovery nurse helps the patient wake up after the surgery and makes sure the patient is doing well. Part of this person's job is to pass out lots of popsicles, crackers, soda, and juice! Recovery nurses also inform family members when the operation is over and tell patients how to take care of themselves once they leave the hospital.

THE RESULTS

Job's voice sounded funny, and his throat hurt to talk a little.

The recovery nurse seemed to understand. "It will feel better soon, and then you can have lots and lots of ice cream!"

"Now that's what I'm talking about!" Job answered.

Is there any procedure where patients get chili dogs for recovery?

Job's school puts on a big play for the local preschool every year, and this year's production of "All Your Muscles Matter" promised to be a big hit. Job's part was the Right Bicep.

On the afternoon of the big performance, Job's teacher told him to "break a leg." "Break a leg" means "good luck" in theater talk.

As Job's luck had it, he tripped over one of the Triceps during their first big song, "Pumping Iron." Since Job falls down often, the other players kept performing around Job, but this time, Job had problems getting back up.

"Ow! Ow! Ow!" he said, which wasn't part of his lines.

"I think you broke your leg," the language arts teacher declared. "Call an ambulance!"

OOF!!

In many emergency situations, it's safest to call an ambulance to get a sick or injured person to a hospital. That's because **emergency medical technicians (EMTs)** arrive quickly and can start taking care of the sick or injured person during the ride to the hospital. EMTs are trained to provide the basic emergency medical care needed until they can get the patient to a doctor.

EMTs coming through!

Ambulances deliver patients directly to the emergency room, where one of the first people to meet them is the **ER nurse**, sometimes known as a triage nurse. It is this person's responsibility to check all the patients' conditions and decide who needs to be treated first. The people who need medical attention the most go first. ER Nurses also take patients' vital signs, set up examination areas, and order tests.

X-rays are important tools used by doctors to determine if a bone is broken. An x-ray is taken by an x-ray technician or specialized nurse, then the radiologist "reads" the images. A **radiologist** is a doctor who specializes in reading images from x-rays, CAT scans, or MRIs. The radiologist prepares reports that let other doctors and nurses know if there

X-rays show pictures from the inside out.

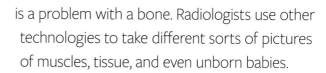
is a problem with a bone. Radiologists use other technologies to take different sorts of pictures of muscles, tissue, and even unborn babies.

Once all the tests have been completed, an **ER doctor** will read the results and decide what to do with the patient's injury or sickness. This doctor may order more tests, put a cast on a broken bone, or decide that the patient needs surgery. During serious emergency situations, the ER doctor will take over from the EMTs and take care of the patient right away until other doctors can come in to do surgery or provide other treatments.

A **physical therapist** is just one of the many different types of therapists found in a hospital. They develop exercise programs to help patients strengthen the injured areas so patients will soon be as good as new. Other types of therapists help people who have trouble speaking after a stroke while others assist those with emotional pain and suffering due to crisis or mental illness.

THE RESULTS

"This wasn't the cast party I had in mind tonight," Job joked with the ER resident who put on his cast.

But Job enjoyed having his classmates sign it. And after six weeks in the cast and six more of physical therapy, he'll be good as new in time for the next school play, "Dem Bones."

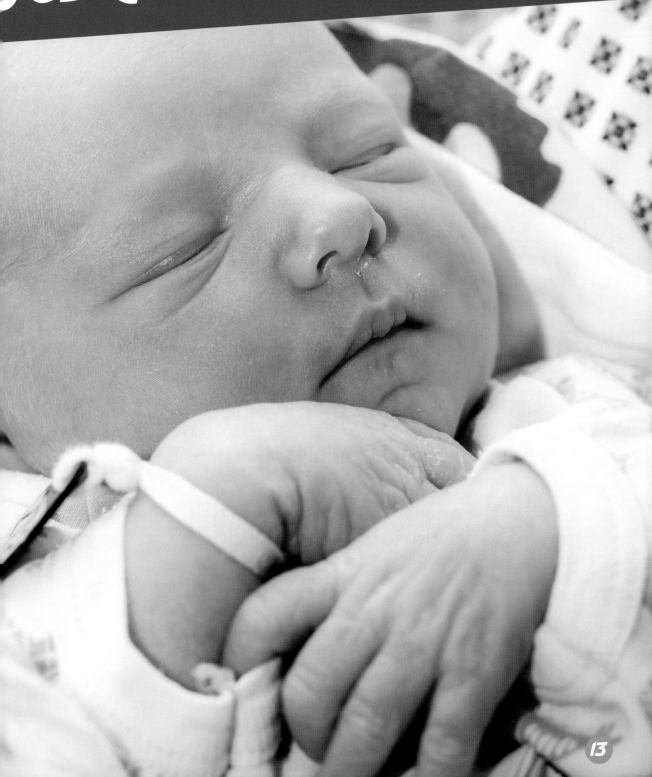

CHAPTER 3

JOB GETS A BABY SISTER

Job's third trip to the hospital wasn't because he was sick or hurt.

In fact, no one was. His mom was having a baby! Job was going to be a big brother! Everyone was excited!

They were in the maternity ward, and Job was allowed to be in the room with his parents until the baby arrived.

"It's about time we found a fun reason to visit the hospital," Job said.

"Speak for yourself," his mother said between **contractions**. "Having a baby is no picnic."

"Aw, Mom, all this talk about picnics is making me hungry!"

Labor and delivery nurses help women manage the childbirth experience. This nurse monitors the baby's heart rate and the mother's vital signs, gives medication as needed, and coaches the new mom during delivery. Labor and delivery nurses also keep the doctor updated.

When the time comes, an **obstetrician** will deliver the baby. An obstetrician is a doctor who specializes in women's health, pregnancy, and childbirth.

This is the doctor women visit during pregnancy for checkups, and also after giving birth.

Some moms prefer to have a **midwife** deliver the baby. A midwife is usually a **certified** nurse who helps women from the beginning of the pregnancy, through childbirth, and beyond. Midwives can deliver babies, but they cannot perform emergency, **cesarean sections**. Only a medical doctor may perform this operation.

Ultrasounds show images of babies before they are born.

A **maternity nurse** provides care for newborn babies and helps new parents with feeding, bathing, and dressing the newest addition to their family.

If a baby is born prematurely (too early), or is having some other problem, a **neonatal nurse** springs into action. These nurses are trained to care for babies with special needs during their first four weeks of life. They help the baby grow and heal during this very important time, while providing families with the information and support they need.

Pediatricians examine newborn patients.

THE RESULTS

It's a girl!

Job was relieved that everything went as planned, and Mom and his new sister were as healthy as could be. After an overnight stay at the hospital, it was time to go home.

Job made sure nothing went wrong on the way to the car. But he was disappointed the nurse wouldn't let him wrap the baby in bubble wrap.

Awww...

POP POP

HEALTH BIT

In the time it takes you to count "one Mississippi," an average of 4.3 babies are born somewhere on the planet. Multiply 4.3 by 86,400, the number of seconds in a day. That's about how many babies are born around the world every day.

CHAPTER 4

JOB'S GRANDPA HAS A HEART ATTACK

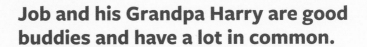

Job and his Grandpa Harry are good buddies and have a lot in common.

They like trading what Grandpa Harry calls their "war stories." Neither is afraid to brag about how big their last accident was, or how long it took to fix up their latest injuries at the hospital.

But Grandpa Harry's latest trip to the hospital wasn't because of an accident. He had a real emergency! Job was playing golf with Grandpa Harry and some of his friends when Grandpa started acting funny.

First he got real dizzy, then he grabbed his chest. One of his friends called 911, and in no time, a helicopter came and whisked Grandpa to the hospital.

When someone has a serious health emergency, sometimes an ambulance cannot get them to the hospital soon enough. The quickest way to get the medical care they need is by air. A **Flight for Life pilot** flies to the rescue in a helicopter equipped with emergency medical equipment. These pilots are well-trained, licensed helicopter pilots. It would be pretty tricky to fly a helicopter and save someone's life at the same time! That's why highly specialized medical crews are also on board to operate medical equipment and take care of the patient.

A **cardiologist** is a heart doctor with special training and skill in finding, treating, and preventing heart diseases. When heart attack patients arrive at a hospital emergency room, cardiologists are brought in to figure out what needs to be done. A heart attack requires immediate care by cardiologists and quick-thinking ER residents, interns, and doctors.

Saving time saves lives!

If heart-attack victims or other critically ill patients are in need of constant care and observation, they go to a special hospital ward called the intensive care unit (ICU). An **ICU nurse** works with patients with life-threatening conditions, and provides around-the-clock care and attention to get patients through their health crisis.

Nurses use stethoscopes to listen to patients' heartbeats.

I wonder if heart attacks are contagious.

A **hospitalist** is a doctor who only cares for patients in hospitals, not in a primary care office on a regular basis—like for annual sports exams. Some hospitalists specialize in specific types of care like emergency care, pediatrics, or oncology (the treatment of cancer).

THE RESULTS

Job's parents met him and Grandpa Harry's golf buddies in the waiting room. Job gave them the update. "Grandpa's still in surgery, and he'll be there for hours!"

All they could do was wait and worry ...

HEALTH BIT

Heart disease is the number-one killer of both men and women in the United States. Three things you can do to prevent heart disease:

1. Never, ever smoke or use tobacco.

2. Exercise! A lot! Go outside and play!

3. Eat a healthy diet that includes lots of fruits, vegetables, and whole grains.

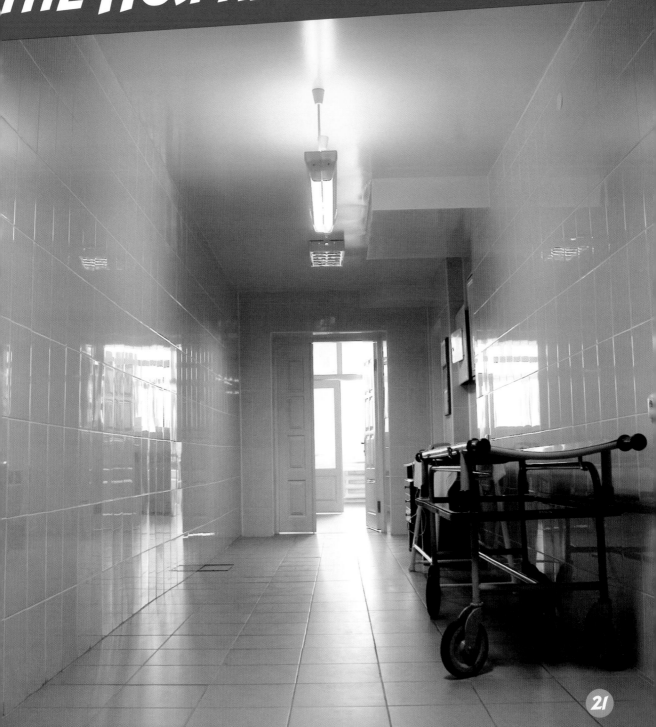

CHAPTER 5
JOB GETS LOST AT THE HOSPITAL

Whew! Job's grandpa made it through surgery and is going to be okay.

After a few days in intensive care, he was strong enough to be moved to a room in the cardiac care ward.

Things were still serious, though, so Job and his family spent a lot of time visiting Grandpa Harry at the hospital. Job was glad to be there for his grandfather. One day, he was bored and decided to take a stroll around the hospital.

Next thing he knew, Job was lost in the hospital's basement!

When doctors order special blood tests or biopsies, a **pathologist** examines the results of the tests and is able to see if there are any problems. Pathologists are doctors who help diagnose diseases and other health problems by analyzing the results of an incredible variety of medical tests.

Microscopes give pathologists a close-up view of specimens.

Medical examiners, (also known as forensic pathologists) are doctors who work with dead bodies. They perform **autopsies** and other types of medical investigations to determine why or how a person died. Medical examiners typically work with patients who died under mysterious circumstances, such as crime victims or accidents.

Hospitals are big places where lots of people come and go. There is a lot of expensive equipment, and many places require special permission to visit. In other words, hospitals are places where **security officers** are needed to keep people and property safe.

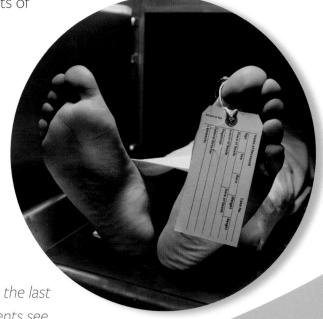

Medical examiners are the last doctors some patients see.

THE RESULTS

With the help of a security officer, Job finally found his way back to the waiting area.

"Good news!" his mother said. "Grandpa Harry gets to go home today."

Job threw his hands up in the air and did a happy dance! He slipped and fell, of course.

Ow!
At least I'm already in the right place.

CHAPTER 6
WHO DOES WHAT AT HOSPITALS?

WHO DOES WHAT?

Job met many different kinds of doctors during his hospital visits. Can you match the job title with the correct job description?

Please do NOT write in this book if it is not yours. Use a separate piece of paper.

1. Doctor who uses special medicines to put people to sleep during surgeries

2. Doctor who delivers babies

3. Doctor who treats heart diseases

4. Doctor who performs surgeries

5. Doctor who conducts autopsies on deceased patients

A. Cardiologist

B. Surgeon

C. Medical examiner

D. Obstetrician

E. Anesthesiologist

Answer Key: 1-E; 2-D; 3-A; 4-B; 5-C

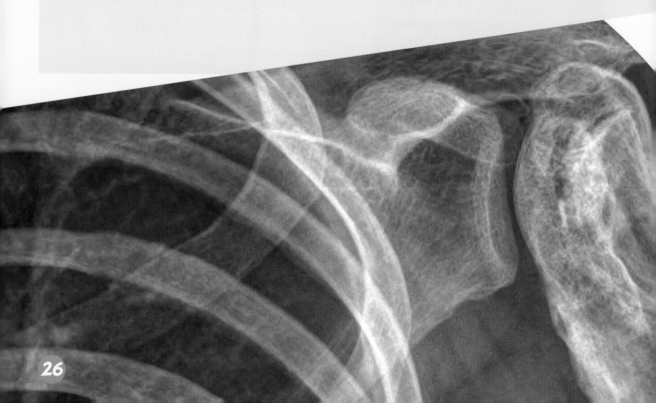

WHO? WHAT? WHY?

Choose the correct job title to complete the sentences below.

1. An _____ transports sick or injured patients to the hospital in an ambulance.

2. A _____ conducts lab tests to help diagnose diseases.

3. An _____ provides constant care to patients with life-threatening conditions.

4. A _____ takes x-rays and conducts tests like ultrasounds and CT scans.

5. A _____ takes care of babies who are premature or have special health needs.

A. neonatal nurse

B. EMT

C. radiologist

D. ICU nurse

E. pathologist

Answer key: 1-B; 2-E; 3-D; 4-C; 5-A

CHAPTER 7
IT'S YOUR TURN

Job has had lots of hospital adventures.

Share a hospital experience you or a family member had. Be sure to mention all the people who helped you.

Pssst ... If this book doesn't belong to you, write your answers on a separate sheet of paper so you don't get in BIG trouble.

Go online to download a free activity sheet at
www.cherrylakepublishing.com/activities.

GLOSSARY

admissions representative
person responsible for admitting patients to the hospital

anesthesiologist
doctor who administers pain-reducing medication, called anesthesia, during surgeries and other medical procedures

autopsies
examinations performed on dead people to find the cause of death

biceps
the large muscle on the front of your arm between your shoulder and inner elbow

cardiologist
doctor who specializes in treating heart disease

certified
having earned an official paper that states something is a fact

cesarean sections
surgical delivery of babies

contractions
the shortening of muscles over a space of time before and during childbirth

emergency medical technician (EMT)
medical professional trained to provide basic emergency care until patients can be transported to a hospital

ER doctor
doctor who sees patients in the emergency room

ER nurse
medical professional who checks the patients' conditions in the emergency room and decides who needs to be treated first

Flight for Life pilot
specially trained helicopter pilot who transports patients to hospitals in emergency situations

hospitalist
doctor who specializes in treating hospitalized patients

ICU nurse
medical professional who cares for patients with life-threatening conditions

labor and delivery nurse
medical professional who helps women throughout the childbirth experience

maternity nurse
medical professional who provides care for newborn babies and helps new parents

medical examiner
doctor who investigates deaths occurring under unusual or suspicious circumstances

midwife
person trained to assist women during childbirth

neonatal nurse
medical professional trained to care for babies with special needs during their first four weeks of life

obstetrician
doctor who cares for women during pregnancy and childbirth

pathologist
doctor who analyzes test results and helps diagnose diseases and other health problems

physical therapist
medically trained professional who specially designs exercises and equipment to help patients regain or improve their physical abilities

pre-operative nurse
medical professional who gets patients ready for surgery

radiologist
doctor who specializes in diagnosing and treating diseases and injuries using medical techniques such as x-rays

recovery nurse
medical professional who works with patients after their surgery

security officer
person who is paid to protect property, assets, or people

surgeon
doctor who performs operations

surgery
medical treatment that involves repairing, removing, or replacing injured or diseased parts of the body, usually by cutting

tonsillitis
inflammation of the tonsils

INDEX

ABOUT THE AUTHOR

Joe Rhatigan is an accident-prone author whose works include *Ouch! The Weird & Wild Ways Your Body Deals with Agonizing Aches, Ferocious Fevers, Lousy Lumps, Crummy Colds, Bothersome Bites, Breaks, Bruises & Burns*; *White House Kids*; and *Inventions That Could Have Changed the World, But Didn't*. He lives in Asheville, North Carolina, with his wife and three kids.